THE VITAL SYSTEM

THE VITAL SYSTEM

POEMS

CM BURROUGHS

Tupelo Press

North Adams, Massachusetts

The Vital System.
Copyright 2012 CM Burroughs. All rights reserved.

Library of Congress CIP data: 2012
Burroughs, CM, 1981–
The vital system : poems / CM Burroughs. -- 1st paperback ed.
    p. cm.
ISBN 978-1-936797-15-8 (pbk. : alk. paper)
I. Title.
PS3602.U7644V58 2012
811'.6--dc23

                              2012020447

Cover and text designed by Josef Beery.
Cover photograph / art: "Equus Caballus III" by Elaine Duigenan (www.elaineduigenan.com).
Used with permission of the artist.

First paperback edition: October 2012.

Tupelo Press
P.O. Box 1767
243 Union Street, Eclipse Mill, Loft 305
North Adams, Massachusetts 01247
Telephone: (413) 664–9611 / Fax: (413) 664–9711
editor@tupelopress.org / www.tupelopress.org

Tupelo Press is an award-winning independent literary press that publishes fine fiction, nonfiction, and poetry in books that are a joy to hold as well as read. Tupelo Press is a registered 501(c)3 non-profit organization, and we rely on public support to carry out our mission of publishing extraordinary work that may be outside the realm of large commercial publishers. Financial donations are welcome and are tax deductible.

*The author and publisher thank the Department of English
at Columbia College Chicago for support.*

ART WORKS.
arts.gov

*Supported in part by an award from
the National Endowment for the Arts*

For my sister.

CONTENTS

I

II

III

All this that I'm writing is as hot as a hot egg that you quickly pass back and forth from hand to hand so you won't burn yourself — I've painted an egg. And now, as in my painting, all I say is: "egg," and that's enough.

— Clarice Lispector, from *Stream of Life*

I

DEAR INCUBATOR,

At six months' gestation, I am a fabrication born far too soon. My body, a stone in a steaming basket.

I remember you.

— [Figureless]

— A black kaleidoscope. Turn. Turn. The dangerous loom of the loom of you. Patterns pressing upon — me inside. Nothing luminous as my mother's womb. This second attempt at formation; a turn.

The nurse slides her wedding band past my hand, beyond my elbow and over my shoulder. I am 1 lb. 12 oz. and already feminine. Knowing nothing of it. I am trying to be clear —

> I was first fascinated then afraid of the shapes' rise from your darkness. And their growth toward me. I wailed under their weight. My eyes were shuttered by lids. My skin was translucent; anyone could see me working.

> How can I ask you from inside the poem — what senses did I have so early … So unformed. I was tangled in tubes (that kept my heart pumping; that kept my lungs from collapsing; food to the body; oxygen to the brain).

You are everything and nothing.

> A surrogate. A packaging of half-made sensory detail; a past.

> I have scars on my belly in shapes of fish … Where sensors tore thin skin. What a tragedy to be powerless. And yet, I controlled the choreography of everyone around me (the check of vitals; arms through the arm ports; my parents' speech; also, there were surgeons).

> I am trying to tell you something important. About after they opened you and took me out. I was infected. Could command nothing of my legs. For years.

The surgeons, thin blades shining into nothing. Imagine the cuts — blood spread along the lip of each, spilling as my skin parts. Someone bringing cotton to catch it.

Is it your fault? I don't know. I was in a state, I've explained. I don't know what you let in … Perhaps. Do you know lovers ask about these scars. Touch these raised scars.

So much has happened. I'm black. I have a dead sister. I love you, but, and believe this, I mostly want to talk.

When he wrote, "There's a glove in the crick," I asked, "Are you from the South?"
He was, more or less. And when I said it, "South"— and why I haven't gone back —
my sister ended up in my mouth. Like a bullfrog. Like cherry blossom — choking.

What sister? What sister.

He meant creek, you know. But I got [the usage] and [the origin] wept. He was my student.
Sweet and smelled like a delicious word. Anyway, the question wasn't so much What as When.

Humble locomotives release breathing cargo, replenish her image. i.e. Resuscitate the child timelessly. View the platform; all varieties of traveler disembark. Strangers escape periphery's clutch. Flood of gratitude: seeing her versus desiring the multi-dimensional, lucid mirage. Morse-like sibling; sum of recollections, she flashes in the near field, cheeks licked with blush. It is twilight. Nostalgia grows in moonlight. Laughter's wisteria shape. *Subjective images play upon the mind.* Rabbit — rabbit till she disappears.

Hawkweed jimmies window seals. Room for a man whose liquor eclipses him. Beg quiet the body. Fight.

                                                        /strike

softly, impact nothing. Even your dream, a woman who allows a woman to die. Leaving from or for the world, prayer beads' iridescent *yes/no*.

Never admit that the poet in you might use it. Wait, as you are cut into, long enough to draw the body's pre-break, the red core's praxis. Drafts of self and self. Deleting.

But he draws back my clothes, covers me
in a palette of skirts and there is a blouse here;
I am less touched. Finally, goodness.

He paints a field around me. My legs curl
under; I am happy here. Great
baskets at my sides fill with: this

is a passionflower; this is a black-eyed
susan; this is a tired iris; this is a bloom of
cotton bright as that sun and that

moon. Happy here?
My lips feather in grotesque smile.
This land. This abyss.

When he is unhappy with
so many things, he stabs the forests
behind me and these bolls in front.

They do not turn away; they turn brighter.

A door. A small mouth at its bottom for vermin, cats, children. Beyond the door, a scatter of rooms. At the edge of it, or the boiling middle, a red window. The sill may be kissed, soothed even. The latch turned, lifted, swiveled—of all the ways to open a window. Watch your fingers, the panes are wet with—you've heard it before. Be careful of your fingers. It is red. It calls to be raised. Don't scathe your palms; this is the scalding center. Answer it. Lift it. You will have no words on the other side. You will have your surrendering hands. The window is seething, is streaking, is—. You must increase your threshold for pain so this does not become a chronic problem.

Mockingbirds at the window;
        You've watered them already, he says.
He pushes years of effects —
        I water them again. I water them —
inside a traveling bag. What falls —
        until each leaf is weighted with —
from its bursting mouth? Must be
        water. Until each stem drowns from
overtaking.

I'm serious, he says, I'm serious.
        The shape of his palm is changed.
His hands   knead an ocean blue
        no longer fitting my breast. When he
cups rice in his hands, I think this pocket
        is more familiar.
Does it make sense that — the boil perfectly
        round — someone is taking everything?

There is this cologne —
        she rises like oil from his temples —
in everything that is mine.
        He opens his mouth and closes it.

I am in the bath fingering bottles.
        Five days no easy conversation.
Borders. Keep them, he says.
        I am building a wall of bamboo.
I don't wear it. *Yes, you do.*
        Almost finished now.

Whatever he says is painful —
        The skin of the conga braces —
I'm leaving the record player and
        He beats and beats it. He —
Kind of Blue; I'll have the yard swept —
        bends its warmed belly and
weeps — *until October.*
        Name of the sound: Run

What covers a naked woman?
        Almost finished now.
He reads a journal in the stiffest
        chair. Underneath its fabric
are springs with obedient
        heads. What covers her.

Once I wrote a poem larger than any man, even Jesus.
So tall the furrow of hair couldn't be tousled,
feet large as lakes. I titled it Personification so it
would live, Godzilla in parenthesis so it would kill.

There was blood. Testicles lay in the streets
like confetti post-parade. I was glad: Diana
after Actaeon's own salivating pack consumed him —
limb by limb licked, tendons trailing.

I rode the shoulder of my poem, wanting to see
their faces, none specific, all malevolent, calling out
last moments in ridiculous language — *love, affection,*
tender, one screamed. Not loudly enough and too late.

I wore red paint, salvaging neither plated breast,
nor firm mouth. Not once was I tender.
I wanted them wasted — him, him, him, him, him

Didactic.

Magnetic in-the-flesh.

Says *you made me. I love blood as much as you.* Then

Turns from noon to noon so we view the Heavy

Button, Blown Glass, Fruit Pit. Good

Lever grows to Yes

Takes a chair leg, table ledge (does it

Matter) rubs her chin against it.

Fresco.

Likes it rough. Likes it

Dug. Says *done right, I am fragments*

Of heaven. Convinces you. Says

Let's have you

Slide your hopeful tongue along her eyelid,

Take her

Between your lips and suck.

Breathe through your nose. Don't

Let go. Feel her graze, her eye through your daze.

Stop. Don't stop. This is where

She hangs. From the tongue, the tooth, the nail.

# of partners in lifetime? _____

Do I or don't I count _____? We, she and I, weren't _____, but were definitely _____.

I imagined _____ her, but couldn't cunt-up when it counted.

He and I sweet-_____ for __, ___, ____ minutes, __, _____ hours … days.

I _____-ed him. He _____-ed me. I think. One, for sure.

No aqua-he's. No gilled-she's.
No Evidence. I wash the
panties, throw them
out, no leftover *look how wet.*
I clean them after I come. Although,

_____ and me, we laid in it. But then, that was love.

I'm sayin, soon as he said *Take off that red dress* … I was naked-golden, tender kisses, round and round and round we go, no *how you doin lil mama, lemme whisper in your ear,* but

how amazing.

# of partners in lifetime? _____

… write "Amazing."

II

You can hear the rhythm of the ache. ·

—William James

OF A LARGER SEQUENCE

My lover has given it a name — a row of thistles at the birth of a field —
now I feel moved to a time when folks like him, perhaps like you, give
kind names to kinetic happenings. Names that acknowledge pain but
don't let it out.

Ten years ago, when my bones were growing, she crept into my bones.
A paring knife taken to me, drawn across my forearms and calves to the
veins' exposure. The veins then, one by one, threaded from my body till
the dressing was done from the bone. All this as I breathed, watched,
and detected first my trepid arousal then the deadening weight as she
riddled in, a tributary on flame. How to love a sister. How to want her
at rest. Now she has a second name. *Episode,* he says. *Eis. Hodos.* When
she was living, I called her—never mind. She is changed. Now ends.
Now begins.

Is marked by triumphant dreams in which, again, and multiply this, she hears her sister's daily notes — meat as the moving parts of engine.

i.   Is so close to the dead her arms hook around the sister's back and she scales each rib, massages organs; flexing, swallowing, filtering organs.

ii.   Liver. *Say it.*

iii.   *Transplant.* Term for *stranger.*

iv.   Is grateful to dream of the dead.

v.   Is grateful to be haunted by the sister.

And a girl and boy inside

A girl spread like force and

a boy frightened of

enjoying it   So in the jaw

of enjoyment The red

blouse still buttoned Or

the preserve of blood on

the chest fresh across

your breasts The discarded

jeans The button wide-

eyed and the zipper a

mouth line Sister, speak

to me after this I'm sorry

I dreamt it like this

Beneath the necessity of
talking or the necessity for
being angry and beneath the
actual core of life we make
reference to digging deep
into some young woman
and listening to her come.

— Leroi Jones

SOME YOUNG WOMAN

Begins and ends requiring interpretation. Folk. Metal
twine choking a length of straw. Slender. Bound.
Flightless. Comprehends herself. Otherwise slips out
of roughly translated versions of self. Has opened for
men — who've harmed with good intention: slapped,
spanked, begged for, begged from. Bruised
nostalgically. Left. Accomplished patterns of leaving.
Exits reflecting ways in. Loved, desired to love
herself. Called a litany of graceful names — strove to
embody them. Tasted herself. Tasted feminine.
Choked. Even glimpsed herself a woman she found
unapproachable. Could not breathe. As a bird groping
a wire. So shivered.

Of my lover's favorite novel is

smoke — so passable . . . his hyphen,

imposed. The last gesture of

my lover's unforced favorite

position unhouses, evolves. Of:

broke her back/broke her heart/

especially, broke into a run. The

rind of each signifying schism;

the soft consonants, his want to

be whole, a threshold: He quivers,

turns from the curdle of a woman,

a continent, a cunt, same sweet

hole; learns the tense sensation

of freedom. Begins, strides off,

dripping the *first* segregation,

I

I repeat baby in my sleep. I nightmare baby, dream baby. And someone cuts ice, largely.
The ovaries are crowded with cysts. The cysts rupture in Jersey, Newark no less. The
woman moves very slowly. This is what she feels. Foreign/ill/afraid, nearly. I am the
woman; would I have known? When I come close I stop communicating; fully stop.
Don't you forget to breathe. This is a break from holding it. The comforted hand. Warm
hand. Incubated hand, forming. Can open. Can close. Can age. *Baby/Baby* The hand
is crying. Your turn to comfort the hand.

The plasma of the dream is the pain of separation.
Dreamers dream from the neck up.

Dead. Sorry, let me answer the question. — Boxed.
Dead.

Your jawbone and a few chips of skull. Yes.
I'm sorry.

I went insane, in the dream.
You returned home.

No. I wandered and bled.
For what?

For whom.
For whom.

For you.
Then memory turns inward.

With a strange, clutching brilliance, and
I go over these scenes and incidents perpetually.
[   ]
Is that insanity?

No. Love.

III

I.

I, in strutting cock stance,
anatomy blazing, phonic, self-
made mid-light. Aperture active
in the jaw, in cambers of maw
guarding the vagina's axis. Light
vying to tincture body systems
rumored only *red*. Man's bleak
reverie — the female constrained
in port, magma, ocher-washed
causeways. The late prism of the
metamorphic world; I trans-
formed: across canvas stretched
white, a black bone bi-continental
collage, a put-upon pace.
Belligerent incubator steaming the
New World's afterbirth. But alive.
But a beginning spectrum.

II.

Jumpseed tangles in orchid's
inflamed globe, frames a scene.
Inches inside, *verde*, ardor; green
atop green vertigo prairie,
tendered crevasse. Yet.
Undergrowth. Her bastion
evidences fable: *he plants his
rollicking root*. Blood lets, not
enough to regret, repent. A body
politic ravels. He hastens her
tinning. Inches outside, series of
labels lie like dress. This female;
chartered, doe-still dream.

III.

Labial. Women grapple-hook women. Plum loaf, garnet welt, milk smear; complexion an arousal-lidded cunt. Mode: additive. Rectum tension; seg-regated jetty. *Please* stutters. Carve the runnel. Diagram bellow. What angle? Sap. Cradle. Ruin. Hierodule on knee-tip; American worship origin. Cuspside of mouths' vivid chroma. Posy-fed, leaking beetle. *Lymph*, weeps Cervix.

IV

ON IMPACT

We watched the bird begin — at the veranda's edge and taking off with mission into the French doors five feet ahead. A red bird reddening. Sexed in vermeil. Damaged. Days, this continued — you saw it. The bird dying for the bird: *how to love the self.* A week at least, at last. The elongated click of its mouth a tension, repetition. The work of watching its attempts to die. The words *please* and *don't* mined from every throat in that house. As much as we were witnesses, we did not see its beak gag, did not see it die. But gently noticed no refrain, no rhythm at the glass — its body or betrothal gone.

for the cyst
inside her.

Curling hair
damp as moss,

she goes silent.
You've found it exactly,
blind but precisely
& push the crescent
heads of your fingers
deep as her vagina's
heart for no longer
than you can stand
the canal, rock
bottom & banks.

Pain, that magenta snail,
Take it, she says,
take it away.

I.

> I was accustomed to being sewn
> open, my muscles splayed under
> sweating digits. My mouth,
> bracketed tug. When language
> failed, there was the body.

> *And his*

> ◦ velocity
> ◦ flattened palm
> ◦ trochaic-metered
> ◦ striking

II.

In running, I came upon you, crawled through the door
under your calfline's truss — pulled myself up ropes of
tendons, arriving quite near the heart. Gazed about your
conjugate system. Adored your inside.

III.

Suddenly, you had a woman in you. I. Who loved. Who
wanted loved. You and she hyphened between layer-
shucked, glow-wrought. Spoon fed syllables under the
phasing moon. She called you *gratitude*. Seeing, seen.
Something given. Pocketed in the jaw, stored, hoarded —
you and she, linked in the grammar of —

IV.

What's amazing. The color of your anatomy:
Slaughterhouse red. Only—the body intact, not even
hanging. All the inside parts (seminal vesicles carefully
stewing) pressed in. I memorize your: slopes, causeways,
wire systems. I measure my breath, disturb nothing, listen
to what sounds like rain thrumming your shoulders.
What rain always sounds like from under cover: insistent
tapping.

V.

She begins to itch. Wants to touch the shuddering lung,
lie against the paranoid liver. She has been so good,
settling for warmth, not daring to reach out her hand into
the screen of veins. But gratitude turned desire, she slips
through a loose skein in the abdominal oblique, huddles
inside the four-walled bunker, for good or ill, waits to be
moved.

THE PANORAMA ROOM[1]

---

[1]

The cool beginning kiss. The drag of us, a wide-sighted hunger. My navel unwound
in a greed of hips. Begun in seam: *Open. Suck. Sweat.* Tension's attention. Femme
a'flux; anchor tousled under turning earth. Suffer the myth of a flooded thicket.

She is naked

Breasts, kneecaps ... all

No accoutrements

And his urge toward her hair

She's missed him

Her lifted mouths

Nude in the brush ... Bodies mapped as embroidery

Breast, Breast, Navel

[Breath!]

Cornerseed unsnailing. Frameable: Cell —
[Couple's blood ballad. Photographic heart.
Brightening tremor.] — by cell.

Nameable.

Yet whines out. Collapsible part-nova.
Go to canning. Unbearable lid of:
ache. Child/Pillar/Preserve. Intimation
of womb: *Pray, be a lean parabola.*
Praise marriage's undertaking, dormant
lineages' lit canvas wanderlust.
Praise ambition *to make.* Night's ballad-work.
Nth stains' hearty shelling. Tilling cipher.

Concentrate on the couple: Quotient.
How he holds her. Listen. Their body chant.

My hair, the beautiful
rat pile, the
glistening tail begins
tearing away in my hands.
I was only catching my hair
as one would clasp
a dog's velvet
mane. But it came away, pretty
scarf lengths in my hand. I was
nowhere discreet. I was
crowded —
flash-pan eyes and
erect pointers.
The norm
rifted.
A woman changing
in public space,
exhibitionist menstruation,
a molting
bird.
Awful — it's
awful — hair, flint-thin sheets
of skin,
small pots of blood —
in my hands, at
my feet. To stay here
or to run? Where to

run? How fast? Which
direction — home, or hospital?
Bald.
Will you
lust after me?
Will I be attractive underneath
shower water, where
the point
came at your feel of my saturated
protein, my weave of weekly silt
and silk
sunning atop my spine.
I'm sorry I can't
face myself, I can't look at you
looking at me. My hair was
license
to lunge for masculine seats like I
lunged for
my friend in grade school, grating
against each other like — why am I
telling
this story — we felt stupid
after the org-
asms, empty, thoughtless.
We studied up,
snuck to sex sections,
read that there were
tools that could
help us to be witty

while doing it — Hh
Hh Hh — we were doing it—
and had arsenals
of sleek weapons intricate
as both our
Daddy's sheds. My
scalp is still
letting go. I am still attached
to the floor, my feet electric fish,
tentacles attached to the muscle
of pain — this platform of
bottle-slick
blondes. Hot
coils in my hand are bark-brown.
What is happening? Loss. Why?
Don't you know?
Seven mirrors
including
the television screen
wiped glassy with cleaner.
I have never
been so ugly as
I am right now. I am mourning
Right now.
Will you
hold me? Right Now.

V

You've jolted awake.

Recall the exhausting day, the collapse into sleep. Though —
a door slams and your teeth grind, or the couple next door
arrive in fight and your ears raise on the first spit consonant.
Dying happens just as your waking happens, but backward.
You are struck beyond yourself where focus comes or does not
come.

Or it is a Friday of geometric heat. Your body feels safe in
the bucket seat of the family car. Your father drives from
the second unforgettable landmark to the first — where you
recognize who you will be alongside a gather of artifacts.

I.

the tumble of   presence—   had I turned sooner had I
bone kissing   my precise destination   asked the correct question
the undercarriage: your grave in Virginia   taste of blood in my throat:

absence   visible before it goes under   was it your face
my precise pain driving as into sludge then breaking   in the earth's face?
against the head of a doe as into surf of rock   please

the doe's body turning— gravity of bone
the question beyond (just) the stopping of a body
rising   Yours   Mine?

II.

Driving to Virginia, with the destination of your grave, I drive into a doe. The eyes bulb gently in their sockets; wide ears bend toward my bumper. Bone and body slam against the undercarriage. Your birthday, nine years after your death. It is 5 AM. I spend the remaining six hours thinking of that body splayed in the road. How long dead. How I travel to you with blood.

Love,

precursor to our shank-less entrances. Nothing strapped at the ankle or

in the mouth

but two pairs of six. We felt ourselves fortunate to have beds and bodies

to lay

inside of at night. Like a man in the female outhouse, he and I tried to hurt

each other

so that the public could not break our skin; we used our canines/birdshots/

live matches/

rope. We wanted to do everything that could be done to us. We used

Nth words,

which did the swift damage. There was a gash where he said "[

!]"

Thankfully, he could sew. I was all new within the week except for the

weeping.

He had to hold my face in his hands and say, "look at me, I love you"

several

times before my eyes washed and it was him again. We strode into

light.

For recovery, should we have underestimated the public, we stored the chains

in black boxes.

Hard in the barrel, liquid in the hunter's palm, in the temples of deer eating
onion in the lowest section of the dell; a stone's saddle of holly; a cardinal.

If the camera is a gun
girls in tiny nothing crash
to the bedroom's bear rug.
Courvoisier splashes their
made-to-pop, powdered eyes.

The girls are told to coo. No one screams so the pines
don't brace. The camera opens up and is not a camera.

The Director's 1st
Assistant is face
down in the punch.
He was telling Girl #2,
You look like a dove,
a soft batch of feathers.

Dung deep in fencepost gorges, tendrilled in the fawn's silk tail; a grave-
stone's quarry fissure; diamond of marrow; porcelain figurine.

This in language he
thought romantic. As if
full of dark sky she
turned on him and said,
Talk to the hand.

Her hand was svelte, a ballet.
The pines don't brace so no one screams.

Who escapes? The hot
rapper with Girl #1. His
glass still intact, if not
ringing. *It was just*
like the club, he screams.

His eyes are wet. His brother is back there. Back there. Her hand
is an encore. The mountain is a mountain, a heap of bound bucks.

Flour moth in lush lush (y' hear?)
yard. White a-quaint-ant asks if

       you Need something?

I am Black. I am
reaching into my coat
(Below Coats) for cash.

This *hello, how are you* —
dialect — is strange fruit. It is
plum-black/broke blood — *fine.*
I'm fine. And you?

      (without answer without
                       pause) *Do You Need Something*

      Punctuated (marked) by visioning My hand in her
      man's (my friend's) coat — My hand gripping his

      (b)ills — I'm getting some

cash, I say.   *From my boyfriend's coat?*

look.

My coat (MY) is here —

look.

      (smile) oh (smile) sorry (~~smile~~ grimace)

I'm sorry. It's just that my best friend's wallet was stolen last week, so—

So

So … (~~LOOK~~)

I'm just apologizing —

just, *adj.*: 1. right in law or ethics: 2. fair-minded; good in intention; impartial: I'm just —: 4. in correct accordance with a standard

(look.)

The harpbone's lunar-note melody places your red hand on your lover's wet breast. Gather lit

mouths, yours and —

      a feeding. Commit to a feeding.

      Enthusiasm evokes

      bones' dilation—simple subtraction of   *frame* —

      Dislike the cave factory. Dislike darkness. Love the foundation — there being foundation.

      Once you were a structure of damage. Named solitude everything except *ocean within ocean.*

Now, in the intelligent transportation of language, there is your hand and her jaw line, their

expectant blood-logged opening.

VI

If the strands on my head all lead to my thinking of my self in all immediate spaces,
I visit a therapist to get out of my head, but say

I, I, I

Primp: the nervous tick.
Performance: please observe.

She primps in the powder room. She performs in public. She visits a therapist to leave
her self with someone else. Repeat *I, I, I.*

I must tell you, and possibly you know, there is only this stage.

I.

[In this position in the poem: a maidservant.]
See: mammy/nanny/au pair, slipping into
tarnish like caviar spoons. This is a corner
for thinking about what I've done—placed
my hands over a series, a collection, of
rouged lips and their melanin-fringed rims.
[Reclamation.] I have faced the question:
What are you? In my dream, I am flanked by
such a number of windows that my limbs are
bound by light. Yellow girl. How do I say
no to that much canvas? As the poet of the
poem, I say No. I say Black. Behind me,
horizon fills with saliva.

II.

I write fuck scenes in which you open your
mouth, your anthems and idols gone. No
Dream, no *Stony the road,* flight to no
motherland. By no agency of my own, your
teeth lose root. Like so: *post-* slides into your
dailiness ... call it *Counter-Culture. Post-
Black.* Fancy it. [In this position in the poem:] I
am strong enough to hurt you. I pry
floorboards and lift out your artifacts. *What*
am I? Do you hate me now?

III.

...will eat you...will chew your nails.
[Consumption.] My teeth in our body. My
body in our teeth. How easily we pass.
There is danger in how we see one another.
In anthems, idols. This I mean of all Blacks,
all Negroes. Hand to mouth. Shoulder to
tongue. Nipple to throat. Crude to think we
could sex *we* back. Thrill the threat of
returning. Bound as we were, natural from
the root, shine-eyed, having lightness.

IV.

This is a treatise on loyalty. My beloved
feature of the Black man is his edge, the
tender shape of Otherness, careful valley of
chain. When he fucks me, isn't he uprising?
Stealing back his mother/sister/woman
bound by light? I let the tension move
through me. Try not to scream. Try to bear
the whip of umbilical cords, breasts and
bone. To be entered. To be exited. I lie on
the cusp of our room. Between.

Once I find the maze opening to the canebrake, I see we
are still quite removed from Escape. You are black under
the chassis … detergent and oil puddling across your black
skin. You are so beautiful I say it, *You are so beautiful. Body.*

I join you, stick my fingers into the organs or engine, everything
so warm so dark I can't tell. I move my hand in to the wrist, fix it
when your mouth opens with sight. Your own wrist, rotal against
some metal; one of us, man/machine/ovary, guns to life. I feel that

we will get away.

You must have in your muscles your threshold of pain.

Said, when the light, hole or gracious hand appeared, *Yes*.

First looked behind you to the macramé of tubers, rigs

and your body's openings, that were *made* openings,

through which slender metal mouths sucked or spewed,

all the black-black, the sterilized tears, the life and life-

lessness of that place.

Must have looked on all it amounted, surveyed the

wilt, rot, measurable ravage, and looked away. What

intelligent sickness.

Rather — what is in front of you answers how the water

and the wood bridge leading to the water signify a freedom

only felt when going under: *Count backward from 100*.

100, 99, 98 … It doesn't take what you think it takes

to leave the body. What it requires is that you admit

yourself, the bleak shelter of your body against

the calm ... 92, 91, of what impresses your optic nerve:

Yourself, woundless. And saturating *that* desire

further corrected colors.

ACKNOWLEDGMENTS

Grateful acknowledgment to the editors and readers of the following publications in which versions of the following poems appeared:

Bat City Review	"& Glory" and "For the Circus of I"
The Broome Street Review	"The Last Word," "Nights' Large Fears," "Of a Larger Sequence," "On Impact," "Room," and "Unpacking,"
Callaloo	"Raving: I"
Columbia Poetry Review	"The Vital System" and "A Young Girl and a Hooded Attendant"
Court Green Review	"Adore the Human" and "Clitoris"
Eleven Eleven (Online)	"The Rest, Abridged" and "How This Ends"
JMWW	"From Where You Are, Search" and "Knitting Bone"
jubilat	"Assumed Savage: I," "Black Memorabilia," and "In the Personal Camp, Eroticism"
La Fovea	"Dream, After Her Burial" and "Some Young Woman"
Oh No Magazine	"—For a Good Man"
Ploughshares	"Video Shoot"
Runes	"Dear Incubator"
Sou'wester	"Baby/Baby" and "The Hand Augmented by the Other"
Tuesday: An Art Project	"Artist's Delight"
VOLT	"The Power of the Vulnerable Body"

"Artist's Delight" was also produced as a broadside for the Pennsylvania Center for the Book's Public Poetry Project.

My gratitude and thanks always to my family (especially Mom, Dad, Jimmy, and Whitney), and to Toi Derricotte, Tomaž Šalamun, Terrance Hayes, Lynn Emanuel, Sean Singer, Claudia Rankine, Thomas Sayers Ellis, Carl Phillips, Natasha Trethewey, Andrea Applebee, Hélène Cixous, John Brown, Marcia Robertson, Diane Samuels, Henry Reece, Tricia Weeks, the late Reetika Vazirani, and Cave Canem Foundation. Special thanks to The MacDowell Colony where this work began, and to Sandra Jaffe, Douglas Kearney, Chuck Kinder, and Diane Cecily, who lit my path along the way. My hands to my heart.

Fasting for Ramadan: Notes from a Spiritual Practice, Kazim Ali

This Lamentable City, Polina Barskova,
    edited and introduced by Ilya Kaminsky

Circle's Apprentice, Dan Beachy-Quick

Stone Lyre: Poems of René Char, translated by Nancy Naomi Carlson

Severance Songs, Joshua Corey

Atlas Hour, Carol Ann Davis

Sanderlings, Geri Doran

The Flight Cage, Rebecca Dunham

Have, Marc Gaba

Other Fugitives & Other Strangers, Rigoberto González

The Us, Joan Houlihan

Nothing Can Make Me Do This, David Huddle

Red Summer, Amaud Jamaul Johnson

Dancing in Odessa, Ilya Kaminsky

A God in the House: Poets Talk About Faith,
    edited by Ilya Kaminsky and Katherine Towler

Manoleria, Daniel Khalastchi

Phyla of Joy, Karen An-hwei Lee

After Urgency, Rusty Morrison

Lucky Fish, Aimee Nezhukumatathil

Biogeography, Sandra Meek

Long Division, Alan Michael Parker

Intimate: An American Family Photo Album, Paisley Rekdal

The Beginning of the Fields, Angela Shaw

Cream of Kohlrabi: Stories, Floyd Skloot

The Forest of Sure Things, Megan Snyder-Camp

Babel's Moon, Brandon Som

Traffic with Macbeth, Larissa Szporluk

the lake has no saint, Stacey Waite

Archicembalo, G. C. Waldrep

Dogged Hearts, Ellen Doré Watson

American Linden, Matthew Zapruder

Monkey Lightning, Martha Zweig

See our complete backlist at www.tupelopress.org